I'M NOT EVEN A GROWN-UP

In memoriam:

the unknown and forgotten children
– of all religions and none –
murdered "over there"
by "the Hitlerite beast"

I'm not even a grown-up
The Diary of Jerzy Feliks Urman

Diary translated from the Polish by
Anthony Rudolf and Joanna Voit

Edited and Introduced by
ANTHONY RUDOLF

Menard Press/King's College
1991

I'm not even a grown-up:
The Diary of Jerzy Feliks Urman

Cover design by Merlin James
Photographs supplied by Izydor and Sophie Urman and Yad
Vashem

Distribution in North America by
SPD Inc
1814 San Pablo Avenue
Berkeley, Cal. 94702, USA

ISBN 0 9513753 3 4

The Menard Press
8 The Oaks
Woodside Avenue
London N12 8AR
081–446–5571

King's College, London
c/o Adam Archive Publications
The Strand
London WC2

Typeset by Fakenham Photosetting Ltd, Fakenham, Norfolk
Printed by The Iceni Press, Fakenham, Norfolk
Bound by Dickens Print Finishers, Fakenham, Norfolk

ACKNOWLEDGMENTS

As will be clear from my introduction, I could not have edited this book without the support and encouragement of my cousins, Sophie and Izydor Urman, in Tel-Aviv. Every parent's worst nightmare is to be predeceased by a child. Sophie and Izydor experienced this, and in the most unbearable way. I know they respect and understand the underlying reasons for my work and why I had to ask so many questions over the years. At last, with the publication of his diary, Jerzyk can echo the proud Latin words of the Warsaw Ghetto doctors who investigated the effects of starvation on their patients and on themselves, and whose manuscript was found after the war: "Non omnis moriar!" (I shall not wholly die). As it happens, those words were written just as Jerzyk was leaving Stanislawow for Drohobycz. Izydor and Sophie have given me as much information as they can remember or can bear to remember. Sophie's memoir was written in English. I have edited it where appropriate. All conclusions about established facts (and, sometimes, unestablished facts) have been drawn by myself without discussion. Even though this book only exists as a result of their commitment, they bear no responsibility whatsoever for the editorial and authorial presentation.

I am pleased to acknowledge the help of other friends, relatives and colleagues. In Israel: Nommi Gerstel, Misha Greenberg, Lea Hahn, Professor Gabriel Moked, Professor Dov Noy, and Ora Alkalay, the head librarian of Yad Vashem. In

America: Joachim Nachbar (who allowed me to use the ghetto map from his family book on Stanislawow), the late Zygfryd Rudolf, and Samuel Norich and colleagues at YIVO. In Austria: Elisabeth Freundlich and Gitta Deutsch. In Hungary: Ernest Beck. In the Soviet Union: Reb Viktor Kalesnik, Ludmilla Maltseeva, Alfred Schreier, Volodya Tsimberg. Here in England: my long-suffering Polish experts, Felix Raphael Scharf and Joanna Voit; John Roberts and colleagues at the Great Britain–USSR Association; Michael May and colleagues at the Institute of Jewish Affairs; Mike Popham, Deborah Maccoby, Keith Bosley and Sallie Ecroyd at the BBC; Audrey Jones, who helped clarify a particularly problematic point; Barbara Garvin, Rabbi Edward Jackson, Liz James, Marius Kociejowski, Tom Pickard, Professor Donald Rayfield, Ken Smith, Christine Theodoulou, Judy Trotter; Moris Farhi, for his 'board-sounding', and Merlin James for his careful and constructive comments.

CONTENTS

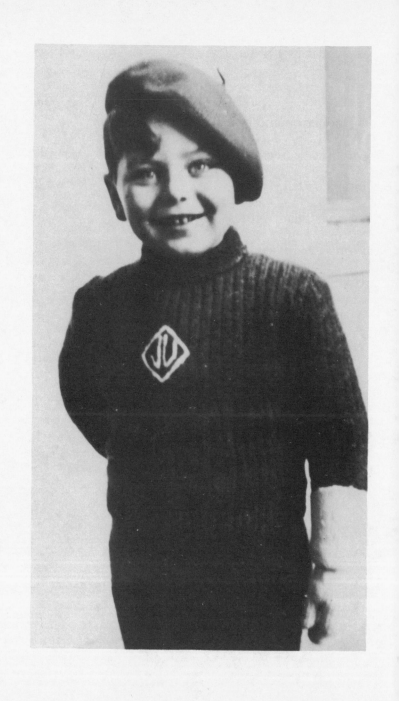

INTRODUCTION

I

Jerzy Feliks Urman (Jerzyk) was born on April 9, 1932 in the East Galician town of Stanislawow, as it was known between the two World Wars when it was under Polish rule. The town was part of Poland–Lithuania until 1793, and then Austro–Hungary till 1918 during which time it was called Stanislau. Since the Second World War it has been part of the Soviet Union and the region is known as West Ukraine. In the early years of Soviet rule 'Stanislav' was renamed Ivano-Frankovsk. The year before Jerzyk was born Jews formed over 40% of the town's total population of 50,000; by the beginning of the war the proportion was nearer 50%. In 1939 1,200,000 or 10% of the East Galician population was Jewish, to which were added 300,000 refugees by 1941.

Stanislawow is very close to Tyshmenitsa, birthplace of Freud's father, to Drohobycz, the town of the writer Bruno Schulz, and to Czerno-witz, birthplace of the poet Paul Celan. Stanisla-wow itself was the birthplace of Daniel Auster, the first mayor of Jerusalem and a relative of the author Paul Auster.[1] East Galicia (as well as Volhynia and Podolia to the east in the Pale of Settlement) was the heartland of Hasidism and the *shtetl*. Jerzyk's paternal grandfather, Fabian Urman, was headmaster of the Baron de Hirsch school in Tlumacz – Hirsch was a German Jewish plutocrat who believed in Jewish agricultural (re)settlement, though

1

not in Palestine, and donated millions of dollars to that end.

The nearest big town to Stanislawow was L'wow, previously Lemberg, now L'vov or, in Ukrainian, L'viv. Jerzyk's father Izydor became a doctor after studies at L'wow and Vienna Universities. Jerzyk's Uncle Emil taught in the Faculty of Law in L'wow. His other paternal uncle, Artur, was the leading petroleum engineer in Drohobycz (now Drogobuch) and managing director of the 'Galicia' refinery there. Thus Jerzyk was born into the professional classes, the intelligentsia, of Stanislawow. The language of the home was Polish but Yiddish was spoken and understood, and Hebrew studied for religious purposes. Between the wars there were fifty-five synagogues in the town. Today there is one. Jewish life survives there for the time being, thanks to a teacher and *tsaddik*, Reb Viktor Kalesnik. Many of the five hundred Jews (recent arrivals – there are no survivors left except for one Bobover Hasid) will leave for Israel soon.

The forebears of the Urmans arrived in the nearby village of Chikhalufka as part of a drive by the emperor in Vienna to colonise and "Germanise" [. . .] his easternmost province with Jews. Jerzyk's maternal grandparents left for Palestine in 1930 and settled in Petah Tikva. He and his parents visited them in 1935. My grandfather, Joseph Rudolf, Izydor's first cousin, left Stanislawow for England, intending to move on to America, in 1903, and that – which is another story – is why I am in a position to tell *this* story, the story of Jerzy Feliks Urman, who died at the age of eleven, a victim of the Final Solution.

The Soviet Union occupied Poland's eastern

2

territories including East Galicia in September 1939, in accordance with the secret terms of the Nazi–Soviet Pact agreed in August. Stanislawow itself was occupied on September 18. Poland was partitioned on September 28. The western part was incorporated into the Reich. What remained was governed by Germany under the General-Government. By and large the Jews of the eastern territories welcomed the Red Army. Germany declared war on the Soviet Union on June 22, 1941: Operation Barbarossa. Within a few weeks the region was overrun. Stanislawow province was incorporated into the General-Government. In May the term 'Final Solution' had been used in an official document for the first time. Readers are referred to Martin Gilbert's brilliantly organised spatio-temporal account in *The Holocaust* of the implementation of the Final Solution. It is clear from all the literature that East Galicia, Jerzyk's homeland, hosted more enthusiastic collaboration by the native population than anywhere else in Europe, the killing fields well and truly ploughed by the Einsatzgruppen and their local teams in the wake of the Wehrmacht. It is the region where many of the cruellest Aktions and most sadistic killings took place, even by the standards set by the Nazis. Reuben Ainsztein, in a book neglected for political and other reasons when it came out in 1974 but properly praised by Martin Gilbert, *Jewish Resistance in Nazi-occupied Eastern Europe*, shows how Jews had to face, and where possible resisted, both the Germans *and* the Ukrainian nationalists. Among the Ukrainians, says Ainsztein, "the only friends of the Jews were the Baptist peasants, a few noble individuals belonging to the minute liberal

3

intelligentsia, and a few surviving Socialists and Communists".[2] Recent evidence from the Soviet archives released under *glasnost* paints an even blacker picture of collaboration than we thought. This was not fertile ground for traditional modes of resistance, though every documented case can be found in Ainsztein's book.

Nearly one thousand intellectuals and professionals were murdered in Stanislawow on August 3, 1941; and then, on the Jewish festival of Hoshana Rabba, during the night of October 12, ten thousand Jews were murdered in an Aktion in the cemetery. On December 15 the Stanislawow ghetto was set up. Things deteriorated further in 1942. There were more Aktions. Part of the ghetto was set on fire in March. Jewish leaders were left hanging from lamp-posts for a week. Five thousand Jews were deported to Belzec at the beginning of April; some of them were marched to the station on their knees. They included 1,000 Hungarian Jews who had been incarcerated in 'Rudolf's Mill'. On the first day of the Jewish New Year in September 1942 five thousand more Jews were deported to Belzec, including Jerzyk's grandfather, Fabian Urman. The next day, in London, the editor was eight days old ... By the end of 1942 surviving *shtetl* Jews from hundreds of villages and small towns in East Galicia were concentrated in a small number of ghettos. Early in 1943 the remainder of the Stanislawow community was murdered in the cemetery and Stanislawow became the first town in East Galicia to be 'Judenfrei'. Jews had lived there continuously since 1662, the heyday of Shabbetai Zvi, and not long after the Chmielnicki massacres.

II

One day in 1942, probably between April and August, in the Stanislawow ghetto, Jerzyk had returned home trembling. He told what he had witnessed on a ghetto street. A German caught a little boy who had been smuggling food into the ghetto. The German gouged out the child's eyes with red hot wire. "The eye was dangling on the wire", said Jerzyk to his father. Without any shadow of doubt this terrible episode in the life of an unknown child (whose *kaddish* too this book is) contributed decisively to the manner of Jerzyk's own death.

After witnessing this action – so typical of the *SS* – Jerzyk, already precocious, was a man. His parents must have realised he knew everything. Up to that point they would have tried to protect him from the terrible reality on the streets and in their hearts and he, perhaps, would have derived comfort from the thought that all of them might survive and reach Palestine after the war. Earlier, among his many projects, he had made elaborate plans for growing mushrooms in hothouses in Palestine on a large scale. According to his uncle Emil he had worked on schemes to save the Jewish people and all humanity.

"I won't go without cyanide", he said when the family was discussing the possibility of leaving the ghetto. "I will never let them take me alive". Izydor had a supply of the poison, a much prized possession, obtainable at a price on the black market.[3] They agreed they would survive together or die together. They would not allow themselves to be tortured and deported – Jerzyk was afraid he would give names and hiding places away under torture, as Sophie says in her memoir. There you will find her descriptions of his death and of its aftermath.

By October 1942 Izydor knew he must not delay his decision to organise a hiding place for his family. Thanks to his brother Artur in Drohobycz there was a chance this could succeed. Artur sent a trusted female employee, Mrs Rudnicka, to collect Jerzyk from Stanislawow and hide him with a Polish family outside the Drohobycz ghetto. That month two thousand Jews were deported to Belzec from the ghetto. In Drohobycz Bruno Schulz had less than a month to live.[4] In November another employee came to fetch Jerzyk's mother Sophie and bring her to a hiding place. Like Jerzyk she had, of course, to leave the Stanislawow ghetto without permission. After a few days spent hiding outside the ghetto she arrived in Drohobycz. Artur, along with some other professionals, was living in a special camp in the 'Galicia' refinery. Sophie was brought to Jerzyk's hiding place, the house of Mrs Huczynska, whose son had taken Sophie from Stanislawow. That night Artur brought some food, a fake identification card for Sophie and an 'Arbeitskarte', confirmation that she was working as a technical designer at his plant. Sophie's appearance was sufficiently 'Aryan' to enable her to pass as a Polish Catholic woman, though of course this remained extremely risky since she might be recognised or her 'disguise' seen through. The Arbeitskarte was signed by Artur's boss, a colonel in the army and an engineer in civilian life. He and Artur got on well. Artur explained that Sophie was his Polish girl friend. After about three days, three members of the local militia with a dog searched

6

the house where Sophie and Jerzyk were hiding but
somehow failed to trace them. The Gestapo had
arrested the landlady's two grown-up sons earlier.
Distraught, she asked Sophie and Jerzyk to leave.

Late December on the edge of town. They
obviously could not head for the centre and therefore set off through the snowy fields. After about
an hour Jerzyk was tired and wanted to lie down
and sleep. Sophie resisted this mortally dangerous
idea. They wandered all night. Next morning,
without other alternative, they returned to the
house. The landlady begged forgiveness. She gave
them tea and bread and asked them to pray to Saint
Mary who had saved them. Every month Sophie
had to renew her Arbeitskarte at the residence of
Artur's boss, Colonel V.B. He and his beautiful
blond secretary were kind and helpful. Shortly
afterwards, having been collected from Stanislawow in a snowstorm, on a farm truck sent by
Artur, Izydor arrived and they all moved again.[5]

By March 1943, Jerzyk, his parents, his paternal grandmother and his uncle Emil were in hiding
in the apartment of Artur's former housekeeper,
Hela, on 10 Gorni Bramah. In the other apartment
of the same house lived two Polish women, Marysia and Genya. Jerzyk's diary and Sophie's memoir
tell what happened in the last few months of his life.

Here is Izydor's own account, from an unpublished memoir, of Jerzyk's death: "The Kripos[6]
came in. Now we knew Marysia and Genya sent
our murderers. They spoke Polish. 'You are Jews'.
'No we're not'. One of them hit me behind the ear
with the butt of his pistol. I fell covered with
blood. Jerzyk immediately put the poison in his
mouth. 'Daddy, cyan ...' and he fell to the floor.

They were shocked and left". Without killing or removing or even reporting the parents.

Overall, Jerzyk had been in hiding for more than a year by the time he died. He was little more than eleven and a half years old when he committed suicide. But even if one makes allowances for his age and for the terrible stresses and strains attendant upon being cooped up in one room for that length of time in those circumstances (his diary shows he knew about executions, round ups etc. and of course he had not forgotten the ghetto episode), even if one makes those allowances and accepts the consequential possibility that he judged the situation wrongly – Sophie describes the demand for money when the police returned after Jerzyk's death and it was Emil's view later that the first visit was for blackmail or ransom purposes – even so, the event under description suggests the likelihood that he was in command of his destiny. It suggests that this was resistance of the noblest and most tragic kind, just as the keeping of the diary must be accounted a form of non-violent resistance.[7] As I have said, Ukrainian, and to a lesser extent Polish, complicity in Nazi crimes in East Galicia made traditional concepts of resistance much more difficult, and often impossible.

Izydor was present when Sophie gave birth to Jerzyk, indeed he delivered him. Less than twelve years later the parents buried the son with their own hands. To bury your own son is rare enough, to deliver him even rarer, to do both may be unique, and unbearably so. The parents believe the son saved their lives. This is a burden. They chose to live. This too counts as resistance. Their daughter Irit was born after the war.

8

III

Jerzyk would have been sixty next year. He is my second cousin once removed. His parents are still alive in Israel. His father, Izydor, is my late paternal grandfather's first cousin, their mothers Rosie and Hermine Vogel being sisters. I learned about his fate when researching what happened to those members of my grandfather's family who did not emigrate to Palestine or America or the UK in time. I have discussed the traumatic events with them several times – and you do not need to have seen the film *Shoah* to know what pain such excavating brings to the surface. My most recent visit was in April 1991 before a long desired pilgrimage to Stanislawow and Drohobycz. I wanted to clarify certain obscurities and problems in the diary. On and off I had worked in, on and around the 'subject' for many years, making notes, drafting poems, reading books, comparing testimonies, attending lectures etc. My regular visits to Israel always included a visit to the Urmans and also to Yad Vashem archives in Jerusalem, which supplied me with a photocopy of Emil's transcription of Jerzyk's diary (and other documents including Izydor's testimony) many years ago. On the plane and in buses I read James Young's extraordinarily important book *Writing and Rewriting the Holocaust*. He would be the first to agree that one should not become obsessed by self-conscious anxiety about formal categories and genres, about theories of documentary versus poetry and so on.[8] Above all one must respect the over-there-ness, the otherness of the material. But that problem will attend a future work in which this diary will have its place in a framework where all the meanings of the word obliquity will have to be addressed. For the time being and in the first instance it is right to publish the diary unembellished. "Right" is an understatement. It is a *mitzvah*, a religious and moral obligation, a terrible privilege. Jerzyk himself wanted it to be published even though "I'm not a professional writer. I'm not even a grown-up". Discussion of certain difficult matters: my own similarities to Jerzyk, resistance to tyranny, the fate of other members of the family, the religious/secular polarisation, the life and death of Bruno Schulz, my editorial procedures, detailed comparisons with other unpublished testimonies, etc. etc., are for the future book.

Jerzyk spent eight months in one room in 10 Gorni Bramah Street in Drohobycz. Sophie drew a plan for me. Volodya Tsimberg of L'vov drove me there, and we were shown around the town by Alfred Schreier, former student of Bruno Schulz. First we saw the various places associated with this writer of genius, and then we drove to Gorni Bramah. We go into the back yard. A small shed is in the right place. Is it the original barn where Sophie and Izydor buried Jerzyk? No. It was built after the war. The well is no longer there. A Ukrainian woman gives us permission to come inside. On our left is the apartment of Marysia and Genya, who betrayed them. On our right Hela's place, Hela who hid them for money and out of religious obligation. This is her room which was (and still is) a kitchen. Then into the next room, with the woman's daughter attentive and understanding. In this room Jerzyk died. That's all. He is himself. And he was one of a million and a half children murdered in a genocide the cruelty and cowardice of which no reader of this diary needs highlighting. It is easy to say that he lives on through this work, easy to say that we died through him in that room. What I found there could have been imagined without leaving London, and yet . . . Britain too might have been occupied . . . We go into the third room, where his grandmother Hermine and Uncle Emil hid. I take my photographs. It is time to return to L'vov. In the car I realise that I failed to say *kaddish* for Jerzyk in his room. This will be remedied in the Stanislawow cemetery. Czeslaw Milosz talks of the pressure of history on experience. In Jerzyk's case both were extreme. Had Jerzyk not killed himself, what would have happened? Perhaps they would all have been murdered in Drohobycz, or been deported to Belzec at once or to Auschwitz later. But then they would all have swallowed the cyanide. Or they might *all* have survived, as indeed the four adults did. Perhaps Jerzyk's death did save them, as his parents believe. This is one aspect of a burden no one should have to bear. And we should not dwell on it, except to say that given the events I described earlier it is as certain as anything can be that Jerzyk was entitled to have cyanide and his parents were right to allow him to keep it on him. And this is all we need to know about the Nazis.

Jerzyk died by his own hand on November 13, 1943. He was not yet twelve years old. His diary cannot be compared with the major published testimonies of children: Anne Frank's, Moshe Flinker's, Eva Heyman's and David Rubinowicz's. For one thing it is too short and too fragmentary. There is not sufficient accumulated detail to enable one to construct an analysis of the diarist's situation and

11

attitude as one could with the other four – all of whom died in concentration camps. And yet I believe publication is more than an act of piety or posthumous defiance. The circumstances of his tragic death speak for themselves, with the help of Sophie's account. Yet there is a great deal of interest in the diary, in terms of movement, threat and rumour, nervous energy, fear, pain, insight. Intellectual and cultural activities in the Warsaw Ghetto and elsewhere were a form of spiritual resistance, an assertion of humanity against the Nazi definition and treatment of Jews as non-human. Jerzyk could keep a diary. To stay alive as a moral sentient human being (and this includes rational suicide) may in a vortex of evil be the only form of resistance possible. The desperate purity of his act redeems us even now – on condition we honour him by working to prevent such situations from ever needing to happen again. This will keep us busy till the end of days.[9]

IV

There are a number of problems concerning the text which so far remain unresolved because I have not been able to consult the original manuscript, which seems to be missing, for reasons that are not yet clear. I have worked from a photocopy of an authentic transcript made by Jerzyk's Uncle Emil in Israel after the war. According to a note by a Yad Vashem researcher, "After what Jerzyk experienced he uses only initials and often breaks off a word in the middle. Many years later Emil filled in the gaps while going through the diary during a grave illness". I cannot always identify these from the transcript. Nor can I check my belief that some of the parentheses in the transcript were added by Emil to explain obscurities. I have indicated these in footnotes. Two other problems. Firstly, after the entry of September 13 there is a row of asterisks and then: no entry till October 24. I believe there may be some missing entries, especially as the chronological part of the diary (see below) is headed "From the diary". Also, attached to Izydor's own testimony are some short diary notes by Jerzyk which I have appended after the diary. After the first four, the remaining twenty-eight cover the missing period. This *could* mean either that the full entries are missing or that for unknown reasons he stopped doing the diary during this period. If the manuscript turns up one day some of these mysteries may be resolved. Finally, there is the problem of the dating of the first two entries. Beginning with the third entry, the diary is chronological, i.e. September 10 till November 12. The first two entries are dated October 27 and 28, the month in figures and therefore easier to get wrong accidentally than a spelled-out word. There is also an entry under October 27 in the proper place. Several possibilities present themselves: 1) the entries were in fact written on August 27 and 28 and Jerzyk himself misdated them. 2) Emil (or a typist) misdated them. 3) Jerzyk wrote them later and placed them (or Emil placed them) at the head of the diary, on the grounds presumably that they deal chronologically with earlier events, beginning with the German invasion of the Soviet Union's Polish eastern territories in June 1941. They do not touch on day to day life in hiding. They are very different in character, tone and style from the rest of the

13

diary. Until I can trace the original manuscript it is impossible to decide whether he wrote them in October as the beginning of a kind of second, more analytical diary (resembling the four referred to earlier) and gave up under pressure of events, or wrote them in August and then found he could only write the other kind of diary. Yet again, the phrase "sketchy descriptions" could indicate that he did write this entry in October as a kind of introduction to the diary proper. Emil was definitely there on October 27. It is not clear from the diary note and entry of September 10 whether he had left the house that day or earlier.

NOTES

1. Paul Auster's family were neighbours of cousins of mine, a fact he alludes to in his book *The Invention of Solitude*.

2. While this savage indictment is hardly an exaggeration, Ainsztein should have referred to Metropolitan Sheptytskyi, the head of the Ukrainian church who "issued a pastoral letter 'Thou shalt not murder' and took the audacious step of addressing a letter to Himmler protesting the extermination. No other ecclesiastical figure of equal rank in the whole of Europe displayed such sorrow for the fate of the Jews and acted so boldly on their behalf". He was not the only member of his church to act in this way. The quote comes from Erich Goldhagen's introduction to Rabbi David Kahane's *Lvov Ghetto Diary*. Kahane, his wife and daughter all survived under the protection of the Archbishop. But Kahane basically confirms Ainsztein's view.

3. See Piotr Rawicz's *Blood from the Sky* and Rabbi David Kahane's *Lvov Ghetto Diary* for conflicting accounts of the poison's availability. Robert Marshall in *In the Sewers of Lvov* says this was one black market trade which the Germans did nothing to curtail.

4. For the only eye-witness account of his death, see *Letters and Drawings of Bruno Schulz*, pp. 248–9.

5. The last occasion she went to have her card renewed V.B. had gone, doubtless fleeing at the news of the impending arrival of the Red Army. Izydor began working again as a doctor, Sophie as a nurse. One day the secretary called out to her in the street. They chatted. She admitted that she too was Jewish. V.B. had saved her life. He also knew Sophie was Jewish but didn't let on, to make her feel more secure. After the war Sophie traced his address, but he never answered her letter.

6. Shorthand slang for Kriminal Polizei, local militia collaborating with the Germans. Izydor thinks they were Silesians. Perhaps they were ethnic Germans.

7. In a major new scholarly study, *Children with a Star: Jewish Youth in Nazi Europe*, Deborah Dwork writes about the lives of the children, both the one and a half million who died, and the eleven percent of the 1939 population who survived. Many of the children kept diaries. One of her themes is the women who were *not* doing 'men's work', i.e. armed resistance, and their neglect in the literature. She draws attention to the work of those women in the Jewish resistance who protected and succoured those in hiding and on the run, especially children. Perhaps understandably she is a little unfair to Reuben Ainsztein. But at the time he was writing *Jewish* armed resistance was neglected or ignored in conventional historiography ('they went like lambs ...' etc. etc.); his documentary celebration of such resistance makes his book crucially important. Let us honour him as a pioneer. Nearly twenty years later Deborah Dwork brings another and complementary world view to this territory, as does Lawrence Langer in his new study, *Holocaust Testimonies* – compare his earlier work in a more traditional conceptual framework. *Kol hakavod* to all three writers.

8. I have discussed these matters in two earlier texts: in *At an Uncertain Hour: Primo Levi's War against Oblivion* and in my 1990 Adam Lecture at King's College, London: *Wine from Two Glasses: Trust and Mistrust in Language*. These two short

15

books and the present one are self-standing, but they do form a kind of trilogy which it makes sense to read chronologically. The long bibliographies appended to the other two directly complement the somewhat shorter one included here.

9. See the two books mentioned in note 8 for further discussion of these issues.

A WOUND WHICH DOESN'T HEAL
Sophie Urman

Again, I am writing about the Second World War. I usually try to avoid this painful theme but as memories fade away with time, I would like to preserve them for my family in the United States. Thank God they didn't experience the war on their own skin. They always ask me how such imposs-ible things could have happened.

I would like to dedicate this composition to my son, who died during the Holocaust.

Jerzyk grew up in excellent pre-war condi-tions. He was a lovely, well-developed and cheerful child with big blue eyes and a brilliant intelligence. He loved me as I loved him and although he was always ready to share things with other children, he would never let them touch toys made by me. "Don't touch it, my mummy made it for me", was his usual warning. Later at school he was always top of the class, affectionate and helpful to his friends who admired him and regarded him as their leader. Even older boys came to him for advice on difficult matters (stamps, books etc.).

He showed an unusually brave and noble char-acter during the war, when he had to adapt himself to all kinds of situations in order to save his and his family's lives.

In 1941, when the Germans invaded our part of Poland they started with a so-called 'Aktion', which meant that Gestapo soldiers went from home to home looking for Jews whom they formed into groups and led to a square or a cemetery. Here they were ordered to dig graves for themselves and then were shot to death.

During the first Aktion my son and I were at home. My husband had been called to a patient and couldn't get back. A neighbour knocked on the door and said that the Germans were taking Jews somewhere. I went with Jerzyk to a Polish neighbour on the third floor and asked her to hide us. She put us in her bedroom beneath a lot of pillows and covers. We stayed there for about an hour in horrible fear. The child said he was choking. I had the same feeling, but I asked him to endure because our lives were in danger. The Germans with a big dog checked the entire building and when they began approaching our neighbour's apartment the woman got scared and shouted: "Go away from here, I don't want to hide dirty Jews". I begged her, kissed her hands, and asked her to keep my son only. He could play with her children and nobody would recognise him because he didn't look Jewish. But she kept shouting "out out". I took Jerzyk by the hand and we went down the steps to our apartment on the first floor. On our way we passed the Germans who were going upstairs and in their fervour they didn't notice us. We entered our apartment, I closed the door and we sat there in darkness until early morning when my husband returned. On his way home he met people who had spent the whole night in graves among the dead bodies, waiting to be shot. Now, half crazy, they tried to return to their homes.

Aktions took place from time to time under different pretexts. During one of them they hanged the most prominent people in the ghetto on the lamp-posts of the main street and left their bodies there for a whole week. When we went to receive our weekly bread ration (300 gms) we had to pass by this macabre sight because there was no other route. No wonder children who grew up in such circumstances very quickly became serious and mature. My son was very quiet, read widely and wrote a great deal on pieces of paper which he collected together. His only friend was our cat Maciek who followed us to the ghetto and remained with us. Maciek had no food problems – the ghetto was full of rats.

There were different Aktions for men, children and old people. One morning the Germans decided to reduce the ghetto and organised a general Aktion for whole families. As we passed the Jewish hospital we saw all the patients, doctors and nurses dead in the yard. It's not easy to forget such a sight. The Germans took us to an old school which served as a collection point from which Jews were sent to concentration camps. We spent a whole day there. In the evening some of us were told we could go home because we were still needed by the Germans. These included two doctors, a pharmacist and a social worker, as well as their families. It was a trick. When we came out of the school, they told us to stand in the line destined for Belzec. My husband and Jerzyk and I stood there for a while but took advantage of the moment when the guards changed and then ran like mad in the darkness.

I shan't describe the details of our return home. Everything had been burned down. We were homeless again. We made several other moves before it was possible to escape to Drohobycz. Here began the second part of our experiences.

We were again dependent on the mercy of good or bad people and felt like hunted dogs. We changed quarters and finally landed in half of a small house. The apartment belonged to my brother-in-law Artur's former Polish housekeeper, Hela, who agreed to take us in – in return for a heavy payment, obviously. She told all our neighbours that I was a friend who had come to stay with her. Of course nobody was told that four other people were in hiding. I had "proper papers" and could move about more freely. My physical features also made this possible.

My new landlady was very religious and insisted that I accept and follow her way of life. I had to go to church twice daily and learned by heart Catholic prayers, the Christianised names of my parents and forefathers as well as a lot of other things, including customs and special greetings associated with holidays. She wanted to convert me into a decent Polish girl in order to save a sinner's soul. I did everything she wanted so that I could protect and care for my son, my husband, my brother-in-law Emil and my mother-in-law.

They could not go out. Practically speaking they did not exist. They almost could not move or speak for fear of being noticed by our neighbours. They read and listened to the radio news, which worsened every time. Jerzyk continued with his schemes and drawings and plans. He said once that he would not let the Germans take him alive because he knew the hiding places of our friends and other secrets and he thought that being a child he wouldn't be able to withstand their tortures and would have to tell them everything.

Through the heavy curtain he watched Polish

children playing in the yard and looked at me with his big blue eyes without saying a word but I saw that he was suffering enormously. He did not go outside for about three or four months. I promised to take him out.

After a long cold winter, spring came and with it a tiny hope for something better. One night I opened the door to the little garden in front of our house and let Jerzy crawl into it. He bent his head to the ground and sniffed the earth like a little animal. "Mummy do you know how beautiful the earth smells?" The garden had jasmine and lilac bushes, then in full blossom, but I could not allow the poor child to stand or even sit up and raise his head. I couldn't reply because my heart was as if in a clamp and heavy tears ran down my cheeks. After a while we went inside and he told everyone that he was in paradise. It was his first and his last outing.

People must have noticed that something un-usual was going on in our house. Maybe we brought too much food from the market or fetched too many pails of water from the well in the yard. Someone sent for the German police who came in the evening and started to hit my husband and the others bitterly. They thought I was a Pole who had hidden Jews, so I wasn't spared. They rummaged around in order to find treasures (money or jewel-lery) and were angry because they couldn't find any-thing. We were as poor as church mice by this time.

Suddenly I noticed that Jerzy was tumbling over. He was very pale and I thought it was a reac-tion caused by fear. We put him to bed and when I wanted to bring him a glass of water he grasped my hand and said only: "Mummy, I took the cyanide". Those were his last words. I thought that I was

21

going mad, I became a wild animal. I ran into the street and instinctively ran to the special camp for Jews, where my brother-in-law Artur lived. The Germans had also left a few doctors alive who were needed to take care of the German refinery staff. They had to watch out that an epidemic did not start up in the camp. I approached the guards and shouted: "Give me a doctor, give me a doctor". There must have been something terrible in my eyes because they let me in without checking my identity and even told me where to find a doctor.

The doctor was by chance a friend of Artur. He agreed to help and on our way home I told him the whole truth, who I was, and under what circumstances I was living. When we arrived the policemen had already left the place. They were somehow embarrassed by the unexpected situation. They had taken our clothes, food, even pillows and blankets with them, and said that they did not take us because they would return in a week and expected us to prepare one hundred thousand zlotys for them, a huge sum of money. We approached the child, who was already unconscious. The doctor had no appropriate medication. I don't remember exactly but I think he cut the veins on both wrists in order to lessen the amount of poison flowing through his blood. I cannot explain today what he really did, but I remember that something of this kind took place.

To our great sorrow it was too late. The child could not be saved. The doctor returned to the camp. I knelt beside the bed, holding the hand of my child, perplexed at the inhuman pains and the slow pace of death of the child of my flesh and blood. I don't remember any more how long I remained in this position. I held my son until his body began to grow cold and stiff, and the pulse stopped beating. It was nine o'clock in the evening.

We acted as if in a bad, macabre dream. It was after midnight when we decided to bury Jerzyk in a shed in the back yard, where no one would notice. We had no tools and dug the grave in the firm and frozen ground with kitchen knives and spoons. The moon was shining and the white snow reflected its light, therefore we could see what we were doing. After about two hours the grave was deep enough to cover his body. We wrapped Jerzyk in a sheet over his clothes and I put a little pillow under his head. We spread earth on him, this time with our hands. By the time we had finished it was almost day. I closed the door of the shed and we returned to the house. Both of us were paralysed. Later I would cry very often, but at that time I was like a stone. I couldn't speak or move and the family left me alone. I took no food for several days.

After a week the same Germans came again. This time they were accompanied by two Ukrainian agents. They asked for the money and when we said we had none they got furious and hit us again. I told them that they could do with us whatever they wanted, for life without our child had no more value.

They looked at us and it seemed that even bandits could have some human feelings. They robbed us of the rest of our poor possessions, but when I wanted to give them the golden 'Holy Virgin' pendant which I wore on a chain, one of them said: "We are religious people and do not take holy objects. It seems as though the war will be coming to an end in the very near future and we have decided to leave you to your fate. You Jews have suffered enough". Another miracle had happened, but a very painful one this time. Our rescue was paid for with the life of our son. But life went on and to our shame we hadn't enough strength to put an end to it in order to follow our child.

I will briefly describe what happened afterwards. Every day I went to the shed with an empty pail under the pretext of filling it with rain water, which was stored there in a big container. We had placed the container on the grave – which I checked constantly, praying that people would not discover it. After about a month Hela took us to the house of her friend Zajaczkowski where I lived openly in an attic room. Unknown to the owner Izydor lived in hiding above me under the roof. My mother-in-law remained at Hela's.

After eight months of continued suffering and fear it was clear that the war was almost over. The Russians defeated the Germans and annexed our part of Poland, calling it West Ukraine. Life returned to normal, even for the Jews. We had more freedom, our food rations were larger, and everyone had work in his own profession. The first thing we did was to sell my last cardigan and my husband's cigarette lighter (things of great value at that time). With the money we bought an oblong case in which we put the body of our dear son. I would not want my worst enemy to see the body of a child buried for so many months without a coffin. Good people helped us to bury Jerzyk in the Jewish cemetery in August 1944. With the money we earned at work we ordered a simple tombstone for his grave. We found his diary among the books he treasured so much.

We spent about a year in Drohobycz, then, after the war, we got permission to emigrate to Silesia. My husband, who is a gynaecologist, worked again at a hospital, and so did I – as a surgical nurse. Meanwhile I became pregnant and gave birth to a daughter. This was the immediate postwar period. There were curfews at night and it was impossible to reach a hospital because of shooting in the street. I was sitting in the living room, around 10 pm, mending my husband's socks. Suddenly I felt strong pains and understood that the time had come. Between contractions I went to the kitchen, boiled a lot of water, prepared the bed, put a blanket and some nappies on the table. Afterwards I placed myself in an appropriate position on the bed.

My husband was terribly worried, for he had no instruments of his own. We had no medication, no syringes. All we had at our disposal were boiled water, a new piece of soap and a clean towel. I spent the night in terrible pain and asked my husband if I could scream. Until then I restrained myself because I didn't want to annoy him. He replied that of course I could yell if it would give me some relief. I screamed like mad and after superhuman efforts I gave birth to a baby girl. We embraced each other and cried with joy that we had an aim in life again.

JERZYK'S DIARY

Drohobycz, 27: X: 1943[1]

Because Uncle Emil has refused to help me, I must begin this written account of my experience of the Stanislawow hell by myself. The hell began for us on 22: VI: 1941, with the outbreak of war between Germany and the Soviet Union.

In truth, under the Soviets we suffered many things,[2] but it was a mere drop in the ocean of unhappiness, blood and tears[3] brought about by the beast[4] of Hitlerite Germany. I don't have an educated memory like other people, who remember every small detail after experiencing the sadistic inventiveness and regular brutalities of the German Gestapo. Some of those details escape my memory, small atrocities which would provoke anger even in a person of average education here before the war. For the average Swede, American, Swiss, the situation would be absolutely beyond comprehension. Thirdly, at the moment of putting this to paper, I am not a professional writer. I'm not even a grown up, only a twelve[5] year old boy – for example three years ago nobody could have persuaded me to set down my impressions.

Circumstances forced me to do it – and the fact that I was forgetting more and more things.

So, for the three reasons mentioned above I am still afraid I cannot paint even the smallest part of the mass of bestiality of the beast-like Gestapo hordes. However, I can say that in comparison with what the other towns and cities of the so-called General Government and the whole of Eastern Europe endured, Stanislawow was one of the places which suffered – the earliest and the worst – the iron hand of Hitlerite executions.[6] If God in his kindness allows this awful war to end and us to be among the few survivors it would be my sacred duty to publish my oh so sketchy descriptions of the massively bad things we experienced.[7]

26

I am starting with the description of our earliest experiences of the Nazi–Soviet war. In the early hours of Sunday 22: VI: 1941 daddy, as usual, was listening to the radio. I was still in bed, half asleep, when suddenly he said to mummy: "You know, it's another war". I immediately woke up and heard mummy ask for details: "What war? With whom?" Meanwhile the voice from the speaker announced loudly: "Last night German military formations crossed the Soviet border. There was fierce resistance. At the very moment the fascists invaded the Soviet Union the Red Army pushed them back to the west". Mummy quickly got out of bed and informed Frydka who did not know about anything and was busy around the flat.[8] They both got ready at once and left the flat to do some shopping in case there would be a shortage of food under Hitler. You must be aware that we foresaw immediately that the Soviets would have to abandon this area and the Nazis would occupy it.[9] We predicted there would be hunger, but nobody could have predicted such dreadful mass killings.

German radio. . . .

From the Diary
execution of orders[10]

Friday, 10: IX: 43

The end of a very lively correspondence before Uncle Emil left.[11] Then Hela[12] or Dziunka[13] brought a whole pile of letters, among them two from Uncle Emil: one for us and one for grandmother. Apart from that there was a piece of paper with explanations, a postcard from Uncle Artur with a quote from aunty Dziunka saying that the correspondence should be cut short. She was quite right because during quite a short period we exchanged over twenty letters and cards. From the two notes of Uncle Emil we learn that he is going for a walk.[14] We were full of hope especially because

Uncle Artur's card was optimistic and Uncle Emil was not going alone but with a serious man who was born there. Even grandma was convinced. There was another reason for our optimism – and this was the reason which encouraged Uncle Emil to make up his mind: the capitulation of Italy.[15] Mummy brought back this information after returning from Rudnicka's[16] where she collected the suit for Uncle Emil. The newspaper did not give much prominence to "The betrayal of Marshal Badoglio".

Saturday 11: IX: 1943

Marysia[17] told Hela when she came to visit her that in Borislav[18] they caught a few people who were in a truck. Grandma immediately started to worry that Uncle Emil might be among them. We tried to calm her down as best we could, but like all elderly people in these circumstances she started to invent things and in her imagination Emil had been captured.[19] But we all understood that those stupid old women were[20] only trying to frighten us.[21] The papers brought news that Rome had been captured. I don't know whether the news is true or not, but if it is, the Italians are poor-quality soldiers if they can't protect Rome. On the other hand the allies would have acted much faster . . . but they don't want to or were not capable. During supper grandma kept saying that she has food to eat but Uncle Emil in the forest – does he have anything to eat? Hela has been upstairs / in 'The Mountains' /[22] and she brought the message that Artur had been questioned because of Melci's disappearance / Emil's /.[23]

Sunday, 12: IX: 43

Today mummy went with Hela to church. When she came back she told us straightaway that first Hela went to Tierstow[24] and that in church they met Urbanowiczowa[25] who confirmed that in

Borislav they took eight Jews[26] from the 'Galicia'[27] refinery in a truck and that even her husband, who was driving them, was with a person of a lower rank than him. The rumours are that all Jews are taken to court/prison. /[28] Hela has come back from Tierstow and is not saying anything. A few hours after dinner only, when we were sitting with daddy at table, Hela came out of her room and said with a stupid smile on her face: "There was information from Mr Emil that he crossed the border and Mr Tierstow said it's a pity you didn't all go with him". After that she disappeared into the kitchen and we had no chance to question her. After a while her tendency to chatter could not be restrained. She came in and started to talk with the same stupid smile on her face. "Mr Tierstow said that Emil was robbed, beaten, grassed on and may be dead". As for the two pieces of information, I did not doubt for a moment that she was taking us for a ride. Up till this point I thought she was sheltering us out of high-mindedness but her tone of voice and behaviour when giving us such important bad news showed narrow-mindedness and that she was deriving "Schadenfreude"[29] from the situation.

Hitler made a speech. It was quoted in the newspaper. A man who broke so many promises and agreements, he is complaining now because his allies break theirs. But excuse me using the word man for the concept of Hitler when he is the personification of the devil: because of the way he conducted the war with his false promises, because he guaranteed the safety of women and children in the civilian population, and despite all this the earth of Europe covers thousands of mass graves, in which are buried millions of betrayed victims of the Gestapo, the institution which was created by him for terrorizing quiet populations and murdering some of their classes, especially the MOST VALUED ONES.[30] And that's why his closest and oldest allies left him. So he will slowly take punishment for the sea of blood which he is responsible for.

Monday 13 September 1943

*So I was right when I said Hela was exaggerating yesterday
purely from a need to "make herself important" or from a
typically female tendency to talk too much,[31] or perhaps from pure
stupidity. But nevertheless we managed to find out that Uncle
Emil had only been robbed and that he is now with the second
guide.*

★   ★   ★   ★   ★   ★   ★   ★   ★[32]

24: X: 43

*The brother of Hela arrived. The gas men appeared but instead of
doing it for us they were doing it for Ciupkiewiczowa.[33]*

25.X.43

*The gas men are working for Ciupkiewiczowa. We found out that
Genya[34] yesterday told Hela: "It's a shame that German officers
hide Jews",[35] /referring to Dr Myschel, a well-known
laryngologist, who was alive, or maybe his daughter, who thanks
to help from his patient – an officer – they smuggled from
Maidanek or Treblinka, to Drohobycz. /[36] Genya left.*

26.10.43

*This poor Ciupkiewiczowa sold one metre of Amerikanki /good
quality potatoes. /[37]*
    *Marysia arrives with her sister's child. She told Hela that in
Rudkach they again murdered a Polish priest and his children.*
    Uncle Emil's birthday.

Marysia Mielnik told Hela that in L'wow while catching escaping Jews[38] they killed two Poles. Urbanowiczowa visited in the evening and said that in Warsaw, Cracow and Loszno they are killing Poles and Jews.[39] At the same time Jews are treated well, they are getting milk and meat.[40] /!/ She said that new militia arrived from L'wow with ten Gestapo men, and because of that she is afraid of some Aktion on the 11th/Polish Independence day./[41] In the entire Catholic milieu Urbanowiczowa was the only one trying to see the misery of Poles and Jews as a single phenomenon. Because of her attitude, she kept hope alive, a rather old-fashioned position, but coming from her, truly felt. Hela went to Marysia Mielnik and came back with the news that there will be an aktion against Jews because the Gestapo has arrived.

Huczynska / elderly neighbour, relative of Huczynski, who guided Izio out of Stanislawow /[42] made sure she got the potato peelings from us for the pig.

During the afternoon Hela opened the window and went to dig potatoes. Andzis,[43] passing under the window, lifted it and broke the glass.

"Don't speak so familiarly to me,[44] I don't like it".

"Don't slam the doors".

"Don't watch me eating from the pot, before the war I used to eat differently".

In the afternoon Hela brought a new pane of glass and beetroots. She started throwing beetroots. Then she went to Marysia Mielnik again and brought back a new skirt. In the afternoon the gas men came and told us[45] they would fix the gas.

The gas fitter is working again for Ciupkiewiczowa. When I wanted to get washed Hela wouldn't let me use the pitcher,

because the water for her hair was getting cold. / Every morning
Hela would wash her mane in very hot water. /[46]

30.X.43

There were no newspapers in town, but there were lots of
Hungarians. As I was washing myself Hela got bad tempered[47]
because I didn't leave her any water on account of the lack of fuel.
The fitters were working for us only, till the afternoon / in the
yard. /[48]

31.X.43

In the morning Hela went to church and afterwards visited
Marysia Mielnik and brought back a cat. The cat wasn't well
because somebody at Marysia's had been kicking him. Hela's
brother arrived and said he had wanted to telephone with news of
an Aktion in L'wow.[49] Uncle Emil cleared his throat.[50]
Afterwards Hela's brother went to the kitchen and started to talk
there. Uncle Emil cleared his throat eight times. At last the
brother went away. When he was still in the kitchen I heard him
say:

> *"I don't approve. Poles are attempting the impossible".[51]*
> *"The Soviets are not so terrible".*
> *"Kiev is being mined".*
> *"In Rudkach there was a newspaper".*

I could only imagine what the connection was. Hela was in
'The Mountains'. She brought some money for grandma but
nothing written, and said there was a panic there. The hot water
bottle burst.

32

The cat mewed.

In the morning Hela went with mummy to church and at the door of 'The Mountains' in the presence of Mischlonow[52] and the girl with the plaits she gave H.[53] various things as well as information that the camp in L'wow was liquidated[54] and the same thing will happen here in a matter of days.

Mummy brought back all this information while I was still lying sleepily in bed. Hela went to confession carrying bags.

She was supposed to take things to Marysia Mielnik but Marysia was not at home and Hela had to carry the bags through the street. / Selling off things gave you the means to live, but it was risky because it drew attention to you. Marysia Mielnik was doing the selling. /[55]

Then the fitter came, not Svk, only the second one, he was working for us. In the meantime Hela was in 'The Mountains' in defiance of our orders[56] not to go there / when an Aktion was in the air. /[57] She remembered she was supposed to get the note from yesterday. Here meanwhile was a peasant woman with butter which she wanted to exchange for soap.

At first grandma sat in the middle room / where if the fitter accidentally opened the door he would see her. /[58] Then with mummy's help we hid her in Hela's room. When the fitter finished Genya came to the kitchen. She was sitting there for two whole hours.

2.XI.43

The fitter came. He went to the kitchen and while we were sitting in the middle room Uncle Emil was moving about. After that with mummy's help we hid in Hela's room. Uncle Emil began to smoke and of course he started coughing.

The fitter said that the job would be checked today, by Fl.

*and some chap from the gas office. But they did not come during
the morning and Hela was asking Ciupkiewiczowa when they
would come and she said later in the evening. And in the evening
they didn't come either. Meanwhile Hela gave the cat back to
Marysia Mielnik. Then she went to 'The Mountains' stating
there were still two more weeks. Some policemen said to Chasi[59]
in Russian when she wanted to go inside the refinery: "give us a
hundred roubles".[60]*

    *Because the people checking the job didn't come Hela went to
Ciupkiewiczowa to ask her about it. She said they would come
the next day. She told her that at one o'clock they shot twelve
hostages for "banditry".[61]*

3.XI.43

*In the morning the fitter didn't come, nor did the checker. Uncle
Emil came into the kitchen and started talking to grandma. When
daddy reprimanded him he got quite angry. After dinner we were
surrounded by our things to sell.*

    *A car stopped in front of our gate and some people got out.
We thought they were the men to check the gas, but only the fitter
came. He brought the hot water bottle which had been given to
him to repair.*

    *In town there was a poster confirming the shooting of ten
people. If by the fourth of the month the bandits aren't named they
will shoot the next ten hostages to set an example. Marysia said
the ten shot already were all Ukrainians. There were two Poles
but the Polish Committee liberated them.*

4.XI.43

*Again the checkers didn't come. Fl. quarrelled with
Ciupkiewiczowa. So we sat in vain in Hela's cold room. In the*

afternoon Hela came back from town and said "The shot people are lying there like cattle." Then, "They will sprinkle them with lime". And Genya, when she came into the kitchen to fetch some water: "I was there but I saw nothing because I couldn't force my way through to the front. First they brought five people and there was a salvo, and then five more".

5.XI.43

"Don't leave any dinner for me because I have a meeting with a lady in town". Later, after a longish time, Hela came back really furious because she had gone in vain to watch the executions. "There was talk that today they were going to shoot a Ukrainian priest and six women". She hadn't even finished dinner when Marysia stormed in. "Come on now or you won't see anything. We must secure a place in the first row if we want to have a good view."

   Hela stopped eating at once. She dressed hurriedly and left. She didn't get home for a long time, in fact several hours. She came into the room without saying hello, and said nothing. We made a point of not asking her anything. In the end she couldn't keep her mouth shut and confided to us that the executions were postponed until tomorrow. Genya told her they were starting to shoot people for hiding Jews. Marysia said while collecting water: "all those women on Gorni Brama". / That was the name of our street. /[62]

6.XI.43

This morning the fitter appeared. He first went to Ciupkiewiczowa's to fix the gas and then came in to fit ours. It happened like this: we were standing with Uncle Emil looking at a map. Grandma was washing herself when daddy caught sight of *some elderly men. He straightaway thought it must be somebody from the gas so he immediately raised the alarm. Uncle Emil and daddy and I escaped to Hela's little room but grandma found herself in difficulties because she was washing and could only run to the middle room. It turned out that this elderly man was the one who was supposed to come with Fl. but came without him, which pleased us a lot. He went to the kitchen with the fitter but they only took the meter and then went to Ciupkiewiczowa. Then they came back to us but only because of the 100 zloty from mummy. At last the fitter turned the gas on and lit it. After a long conversation he finally left and we were able to return. Meanwhile the moment we got to the kitchen someone knocked at the window. The three of us ran away immediately but grandma stayed. Afterwards it turned out it was Hela. She had gone to watch the executions while the fitter was doing his job and came back in a bad mood because once again nothing happened.*

7.XI.43

Sixteen women were taken to Bronica.[63] In Dolina they hanged six tartars.

8.XI.43 Monday

Marysia and Genya engaged in blackmail because they didn't have gas. Urbanowiczowa came and calmed them down. Hela is having a discussion on religious matters. "Keep out of it mother".[64]

9.XI.43[65]

[no entry]

What will happen tomorrow? Pussy came.[66]

Nothing happened. They are taking Ukrainians into the army.

Urbanowiczowa had a dream that "the young woman" was quarrelling with her husband about the milk.
The stupid old women[67] *are having gas installed.*

JERZYK'S NOTES[68]

10 September	*Uncle Emil went to Sandor Wolf.[69] Capitulation of Italy.*
11 September	*Marysia tells Hela in Borislav they caught eight Jews in a car.*
12 September	*Urbanowiczowa confirmed it. Uncle Artur was questioned. Hela told us about Uncle Emil.*
13 September	*It wasn't too bad. Emil's life was saved.*
14 September	*Tle[70] sending info about Uncle Emil. Last of fuel.*
15 September	*Poster. Reaction of Hela.*
17 September	*Marysia sees my legs when she brings in the scales to weigh flour.[71]*
20 September	*Peasant came.*
23 September	*Uncle Artur sends a letter of Uncle Emil. Grandma is deeply distressed.*
27 September	*Night. Emil[72] came.*
28 September	*Hania[73] informs that Auntie Dziunka wants to see mummy or Marysia.*
29 September	*Marysia comes in, in tears.*
30 September	*Jewish New Year.*
1 October	*All three departed.*
2 October	*When Marysia made coffee she heard Emil cough.[74]*
3 October	*Janek, Hela's brother, arrived. Janek hears daddy and Uncle Emil. Hela is back.*
5 October	*Marysia frightens Hela and asks about Uncle Emil.*

6 October	Mich[75] disappears. J gossips about it.
7 October	Dr Getlinger disappeared.
8 October	Erev[76] Yom Kippur. Disagreement. Urbanowicz wants to connect the gas.
9 October	Yom Kippur. Everyone fasted till evening. Story with Hela and candle. Abracadabra.
10 October	(Sunday) Hela heard from Marysia that Getlinger was caught and killed. Afternoon. Panic.[77] Genya came.
11 October	Marysia went away.
12 October	Anniversary of first Aktion in Stanislawow.[78]
13 October	Urbanowicz came with gas fitters. Digging in our yard.
14 October	Urbanowiczowa came twice. Mich[79] was caught. They are digging for potatoes.
15 October	Wrangle. Emil moved while Genya was fetching water. On the eighth[80] she quarrels with Hela because Chasia[81] told her not to take the ticket for the food rations. Strange advice perhaps a warning. Chasia has figured out that we will pay anything for food. Hela behaves crazily.
16 October	Nothing important.
17 October	Genya came in the morning and saw the wash bowl Emil is using in the kitchen. He starts to move again.
18 October	They are going to dig close to our house. Hela went to town. We are unprotected.
21 October	Genya is frightening Hela with the news that they killed 500 Christians in Warsaw for one general[82] killed. The gas fitters start working again. Ciupkiewiczowa's gas is fitted.
23 October	Marian's birthday.[83] Poster again announcing in Sambor[84] that they will shoot Poles and Ukrainians for hiding Jews.[85] The gas fitters get drunk.

NOTES

1. See introduction for a discussion about the dating of the first two entries.

2. A note on Emil's transcript, the only one of its kind, says that the manuscript was smudged at this point but he's fairly sure it reads "under . . . many things".

3. Probably an accidental echo of Churchill's speech of May 1940.

4. A common image in Holocaust literature. See also David Grossman's novel, *See Under: Love*, especially section I, 'Momik'. Momik is preoccupied with what happened "over there". Section II, for those who have not read this extraordinary book, is called 'Bruno', and is 'about' Bruno Schulz.

5. In fact, eleven year old. Transcription error, or Jerzyk's own?

6. See my introduction for a discussion of Stanislawow. Jerzyk is right.

7. Many diaries were kept in the ghettos, camps, villages etc of occupied Europe. Given the large number which were found, we will never know how many have disappeared for ever. To tell the world posthumously what had happened was the passion of many people, including Jerzyk. See James Young on diaries. Jerzyk's use of the word "few" suggests a very clear and, indeed, prescient, awareness that the Nazi aim was genocide. Unless the final sentence of the next entry contradicts my suggestion.

8. They are in the flat in Passage Olympia, 16 Sobieski St, in Stanislawow. Passage Olympia looks very much now as

40

it must have done then. Frydka was the maid. They lived there until they had to go to the ghetto.

9. See introduction.

10. The phrase "German radio ..." appears to be the beginning of a new paragraph in the entry dated 28:X. The transcript then has the heading "From the Diary" (see my introduction). Immediately after this is a phrase hanging in the air "execution of orders".

11. In an attempt to escape to Hungary. See Jerzyk's first diary note, and my note 69.

12. Former housekeeper of Artur. Polish. For all her faults the family trusted her, and remained in touch with her after the war. She died in Cracow in the fifties.

13. Dziunka, the wife of Artur. She now lives in Paris. Her son, mentioned in Jerzyk's notes later, lives in California.

14. "Going for a walk" is Jerzyk's code for "attempting to escape across the border with Hungary". Jerzyk encoded various names etc. for security reasons. See note 23. The early part of this entry is not yet clear to me.

15. On the same date as this entry Anne Frank reports the same news with the same optimism as Jerzyk. Anne Frank had been listening to the Dutch service of the BBC. Maybe Jerzyk had been listening to the Polish service as well as reading about the news in the paper.

16. Employee of Artur, trusted friend of Hela. See introduction.

17. Marysia Mielnik and Genya who lived in the rooms in the other flat in 10 Gorni Bramah are believed by the Urmans to have betrayed them to the authorities, undoubtedly in the hope of monetary recompense.

18. Borislav: a few kilometres south-west of Drohobycz.

41

19. Reading this kind of comment one is amazed to recall that Jerzyk was only eleven.

20. "Stupid old women": if this refers, as it must, to any two out of Marysia, Genya and Hela, it suggests that the neighbours already knew about the fugitives, who knew they knew.

21. Literally: "put rats into our bellies".

22. 'The Mountains' was an oil refinery. See introduction about Uncle Artur. This is the first phrase between oblique lines in the manuscript. I am not sure if it is Emil's or Jerzyk's phrase.

23. /Emil's/. I think this must be Emil's explanation, i.e. that Emil *is* Melci, Jerzyk's code. Elsewhere Emil is named and his disappearance is coded. See note 14.

24. Chief chauffeur at the refinery.

25. Her husband worked under Artur. He may have owned Hela's apartment where Jerzyk and family were hiding. The other apartment or the house was owned by Ciupkewiczowa. Later Jerzyk is very complimentary about Urbanowiczowa's attitude.

26. Here, as elsewhere Jerzyk uses "J" for Jews, as part of his code to fool an unauthorised reader.

27. See introduction.

28. Emil's or Jerzyk's own clarification?

29. Jerzyk's own word, its use being a telling sign of his intellectual precosity. Quotation marks in the transcript – Jerzyk's or Emil's, I don't know.

30. In capital letters in the original. Presumably the professional and intellectual groups. Jerzyk would have remembered what happened in Stanislawow in August 1941 (see

introduction) and known of other examples. Perhaps he knew about Bruno Schulz in Drohobycz. Most likely he did not. This is a case of editor's fantasy, the unconscious desire to "improve" the story as in a novel. Schulz may have been personally known to Emil. He is mentioned in Emil's unpublished testimony.

31. I am not entirely clear in my mind if this is merely a typical male prejudice or Jerzyk's own generalisation based upon close and accurate observation of Hela and the two neighbours Marysia and Genya.

32. See introduction.

33. Probable owner of the house.

34. One of the two neighbours in the other apartment in the house.

35. "J" used.

36. This is surely an interpolation by Emil.

37. Probably Jerzyk's explanation.

38. Here he uses the full word, not "J". Also, see Leon Wells' important book on the Janowska camp in L'wow. His diary entry for October 26 begins: "There is now no doubt that the entire camp is being liquidated." The revolt and escape of the surviving Jews took place on November 19.

39. Uses "J".

40. The very rumour sounds like one of the many deceptions perpetrated by Germany as a matter of high policy to lull Jews not yet deported or captured into a false sense of relative security. The exclamation mark immediately following is surely Emil's. Jerzyk might have been well enough sussed to know it wasn't true but he wouldn't, in this case, have needed an exclamation mark.

41. Probably Emil's.

42. This must be Emil's note as Jerzyk would have said "daddy". Izydor is never, and was never, known as "Izio". Perhaps a transcription error.

43. Unknown.

44. Literally: "Don't say 'thou' to me" (Polish: *wy*).

45. That is, presumably, Sophie.

46. Jerzyk's parenthesis. I think he would be more likely than Emil to use the word 'mane'.

47. Literally 'had flies in her nose'.

48. Could be Jerzyk's or Emil's.

49. No hint of this in Leon Wells.

50. The previous reference to Emil in the diary was on September 13 when they learn he is safe with the guide. But in the notes of Jerzyk we learn (see later) that Emil has returned to the family. Obviously his attempt to escape to Hungary failed.

51. Lit. "Jumping at the sun with their hoes".

52. Unknown.

53. I have triple checked the Polish syntax of this sentence and it cannot be made to mean anything other than what it apparently says, namely that Hela gave an unknown "H" various things.

54. See note 38.

55. Insertion certainly made by Emil. The Urmans believe, with good reason, that Marysia and Genya betrayed them. It is not entirely clear if Marysia and Genya

guessed what Hela was doing or if they were in on the secret. I now suspect the latter.

56. "Orders" is a strong word, and an interesting one. Does it reflect her lower status as Artur's former housekeeper, despite the fact that she holds the cards? On the other hand if it became known she was hiding Jews she too could have been in big trouble, so the cards were not so strong. The word also suggests – though I run the risk here as elsewhere of overinterpretation – that her presence was that of a human being who was hiding them out of religious belief and not merely for the money she was paid, even though she hoped they would convert after the war. But cf. Jerzyk's view in the entry for September 12.

57. Probably Jerzyk's insertion.

58. Ditto.

59. Chasi could be a transcription error for Hela, since Jerzyk appears to know the person. But see note 81.

60. The colloquial Russian word used was "Sotku", accusative form of "Sotka".

61. "Banditism" in Polish: an invented word.

62. Jerzyk's.

63. Local forest used by the Germans for murder. Fifteen thousand people are buried in mass graves, eleven thousand of them Jews. The Mayor of Drohobycz is thought to be in favour of a memorial. In October 1991 a memorial was unveiled at Babi Yar.

64. It is interesting that Jerzyk quotes snatches of conversation without prefacing them with an indication of the speaker. In this instance, as it happens, it could be either himself or one of the neighbours talking to the older "mother", Urbanowiczowa. One dare not read too

much into his language, but the pressure of events upon his mind is clearly released as linguistic energy. The movement of sentences in, for example the entry for November 6 is very different from the first entry. This is a further reason for arguing in favour of a transcription error, and dating the first two entries as August rather than late October. Until the original turns up one must rely on serious reading of the given words.

65. This is the only occasion where the transcript gives a date without an entry.

66. Jerzyk loved the cat, a living creature he could bestow affection on.

67. Polish word: 'klemp'. Cf. Yiddish, glomp.

68. See introduction about the dates. In some of the entries in this section there are a large number of insertions between / / marks. I have edited these out for the time being, to simplify the reading.

69. This name is, apparently, Jerzyk's code for Hungary. Sandor Wolf does not exist: which accounts for why someone of that name in the Budapest directory did not answer my letter, written before Izydor clarified the reference.

70. 'Tle' is obscure.

71. See note 55. Not hard to guess the secret, even if they *weren't* in the know. See also note 20 and the diary entry for September 11, less than a week before the note of Jerzyk's the present note of mine glosses. It is impossible to establish the exact date they found out about the fugitives.

72. See note 50.

73. "Hania" sounds like "Genya" and even if it is a misprint for Hela the rest of the entry suggests that the "klemp" were in the know.

74. See note 71. Also, in this instance, presumably, either Marysia makes a comment, or Jerzyk is assuming she hears the cough. Did Hela swear them to secrecy, perhaps offer them some money? I think, on balance, they found out by accident. Hela's brother (see Jerzyk's diary note for October 3) could have been in on the betrayal too.

75. Dr Mischel.

76. 'Erev' ('eve'), in Hebrew in the original. Jewish festivals begin the night before. See *Lvov Ghetto Diary* for Rabbi Kahane's account of Yom Kippur in 1943 while he was in hiding in the Ukrainian Archbishop's palace. In the sewers too, Yom Kippur was being observed (see *In the Sewers of Lvov*).

77. In fact Dr Getlinger survived. After the war he got to Brazil and "was given a villa to live in by the millionaire Schazman from Borislav." Emil says there was no panic but maybe, we may speculate, Jerzyk panicked unnoticed.

78. Second anniversary. Not the first Aktion, but the worst. See introduction.

79. See note 75.

80. Perhaps a reference to the disagreement referred to on October 8.

81. Chasia, who appears to be Hela earlier, cannot be her, given the context of this reference. Could it be the first name of Ciupkiewiczowa?

82. This refers to an assassination by the Polish underground, and the consequent reprisal.

83. Jerzyk's cousin. See note 13.

84. Sambor is about thirty miles north west of Drohobycz. By this time the town had been declared *Judenrein* after

the usual mass murders and atrocities. In 1944 Jews who had been in hiding were found and executed. The *Encyclopaedia Judaica* does not record the fate of their hosts, assuming some actually were hidden by Poles.

85. Jerzyk does not say how he knows about this poster. Presumably he overheard Marysia/Genya telling Hela. The reason they would have told Hela was to draw attention to the danger she was courting – and by extension or implication themselves – with the further implication that a monetary value should be placed upon this danger. It is indeed the case that anyone found harbouring a Jew would be publicly hanged. If you changed your mind about hiding someone and chucked them out and they were captured, under torture they might reveal who had sheltered them. What to do? One solution was to murder them yourself. In the cemetery at Stanislawow there is a grave apart from the regular ones, close to the mass grave of the victims of Aktions. Reb Viktor Kalesnik explained to me that it is the only one of its kind because the dead did not die in an Aktion. A woman and her four children were being hidden by a Pole who, one day, cognisant of the risks attendant both upon hiding them and throwing them out, murdered two of the children. Before the job could be completed the woman fled and then killed herself and the other two children. This is their grave.

BIBLIOGRAPHY

In the writing or editing or translating of all sections of this book I have drawn on 1) unpublished texts by Sophie Urman, 2) the testimonies of Dr Izydor Urman and Dr Emil Urman deposited in Yad Vashem, 3) the comments on those testimonies made by Yad Vashem researchers. I have also drawn on several entries in the *Encyclopaedia Judaica* and read or consulted the following books. (See also note eight on page 15).

R. Ainsztein, *Jewish Resistance in Nazi-occupied Eastern Europe*, Elek, London 1974.

Y. Arad & others (ed.), *Documents on the Holocaust*, Yad Vashem, Jerusalem 1981.

P. Auster, *The Invention of Solitude*, Sun Books, New York 1982.

J. Bauman, *Winter in the Morning*, Pavanne, London 1987.

M. Cornwall (ed.), *The Last Years of Austro-Hungary*, Univ. Exeter Press, 1990.

D. Dwork, *Children with a Star: Jewish Youth in Nazi Europe*, Yale U.P., 1991.

M. Flinker, *Young Moshe's Diary*, Yad Vashem, 1965.

A. Frank, *The Diary of Anne Frank*, Pan Books, London, 1984.

P. Friedman, *Roads To Extinction*, Jewish Pubn. Society of America, Boston 1980.

M. Gilbert, *The Jews of Russia: their History in Maps & Photographs*, NCSJUKI, London 1976.

M. Gilbert, *Atlas of the Holocaust*, Michael Joseph, London 1982.

M. Gilbert, *Jewish History Atlas* (3rd edn), Weidenfeld and Nicolson, London 1985.

M. Gilbert, *The Holocaust (The Jewish Tragedy)*, Fontana/Collins, London 1987.

M. Greenberg, *Graves of Tsaddikim in Russia*, Shamir, Jerusalem 1989.

D. Grossman, *See Under: Love*, Jonathan Cape, London 1990.

E. Heyman, *The Diary of Eva Heyman*, Shapolsky, New York 1988.

R. Hilberg, *The Destruction of the European Jews*, Holmes and Maier, London 1985.

D. Kahane, *Lvov Ghetto Diary*, Univ. Massachusetts Press, Amhurst 1990.

L. Langer, *Holocaust Testimonies*, Yale U.P., 1991.

P. R. Magocsi, *Ukraine: a Historical Atlas*, Univ. Toronto Press, 1987.

M. Marrus, *The Holocaust in History*, Weidenfeld and Nicolson, London 1988.

R. Marshall, *In the Sewers of Lvov: the Last Sanctuary from the Holocaust*, Collins, London 1990.

C. Milosz, *The Witness of Poetry*, Harvard Univ. Press, 1983.

T. Muirhead, *Out of the Ashes*, Robert Hale, London 1941.

C. Ozick, *The Shawl*, Jonathan Cape, London 1991.

C. Ozick, *The Messiah of Stockholm*, Andre Deutsch, London 1987.

B-C. Pinchuk, *Shtetl Jews under Soviet Rule: Eastern Poland on the Eve of the Holocaust*, Blackwell, Oxford 1990.

P. Rawicz, *Blood from the Sky*, Chatto and Windus, London 1981.

E. Roith, *The Riddle of Freud*, Tavistock, London 1987.

J. Roth, *Tarabas: A Guest on Earth*, Chatto and Windus, London 1987.

D. Rubinowicz, *The Diary of David Rubinowicz*, Blackwood, Edinburgh 1981.

A. Rudolf, *At an Uncertain Hour: Primo Levi's War against Oblivion*, The Menard Press, London 1990.

A. Rudolf, *Wine from Two Glasses: the Adam Lecture for 1990*, Adam Archive Publications, Kings College, London 1991.

B. Schulz, *Sanatorium under the Sign of the Hourglass*, Picador, London 1979.

B. Schulz, *Street of Crocodiles*, Picador, London 1980.

B. Schulz, *Letters & Drawings* (ed. J. Ficowski), Harper and Row, New York 1988.

L. Wells, *The Death Brigade (The Janowska Road)*, Holocaust Library, New York 1978.

H. White, *The Content of Form: Narrative Discourse and Historical Representation*, Johns Hopkins University Press, Baltimore 1989.

H. White, *Metahistory: The Historical Imagination in Nineteenth-Century Europe*, Johns Hopkins University Press, Baltimore 1975.

M. Winick (ed.), *Hunger Disease: Studies by the Jewish Physicians in the Warsaw Ghetto*, Wiley-Interscience, New York 1974.

J. Young, *Writing and Rewriting the Holocaust: Narrative and the Consequences of Interpretation,* Indiana Univ. Press 1990.

———, *The Black Book of Polish Jewry*, American Federation for Polish Jews, New York 1943.

GHETTO AREA
Summer 1942

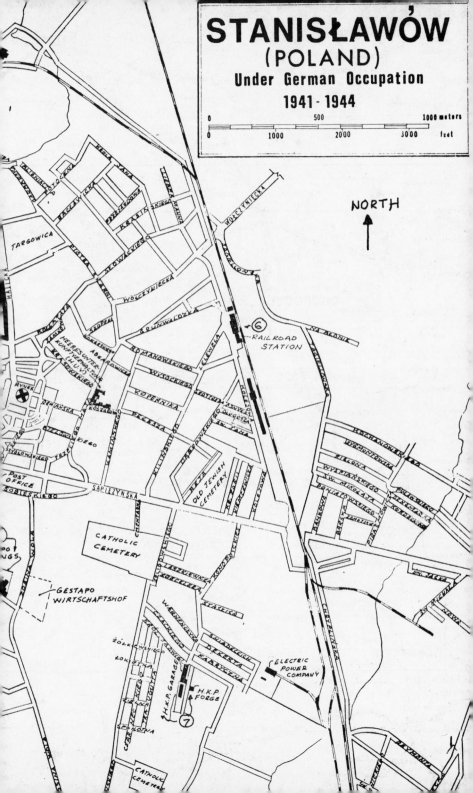

STANISŁAWÓW
(POLAND)
Under German Occupation
1941 - 1944

NORTH

TARGOWICA

RAILROAD STATION

RYNEK

POST OFFICE

SAPIEŻYŃSKA

OLD JEWISH CEMETERY

CATHOLIC CEMETERY

GESTAPO WIRTSCHAFTSHOF

HEERESUNTERKUNFTVERWALTUNG (H.U.V.)

ELECTRIC POWER COMPANY

H.K.P. GARAGES

H.K.P. FORGE

CATHOLIC CEMETERY

LUBLIN
Plask 21 24 45 Cleim
Niedrzwica 28 Krasnystaw
Duza L'uboml' Turijsk Kivercy Kostopol'
Kraśnik Vladimir- 46 Luck 29
Volynskij Torcin 48 ЛУЦК 47 Klevan 23 Rovno
Szczebrzeszyn Janów 34 Novovolynsk 13 53 Mlinov РОВНО 66
Lub. E81 Tomaszów Pavlovka 48 Zdolbunov Go
Biłgoraj Lub. Sokal' Gorochov Dubno Ostrog
ЧЕРВОНОГРАД 16 Berestečko 52 Kunev
Cleśanów Cervonograd 219 Verba 39 Izjasl
Leżajsk 25 Rava- Radechov Červonoarmejsk Kremenec 43 Jampol'
Sieniawa Russkaja 43 10 Brody 24 Višnevec 34 Ba
Jarosław 33 Kamenka 28 Podkamen' 27 Zbaraž Chm
E22 35 Nesterov Bugskaja 31 2 Olesko Podvolč ХМЕЛЬ
ZESZÓW 339 17 Radymno 13 27 Jarovov Busk Zoločev Zborov 24 42
Przemyśl 19 Gorodok 29 L'VOV 57 37 Zbarov Ternopol' Podvolč
69 Mostiska ЛЬВОВ 45 13 Peremyšljany 36 ТЕРНОПОЛЬ
Domaradz Rudki 38 Komarno Kozova 32 Terebovlja
Chyrov Sambor Nikolajev 32 Berežany Podgajcy 27 Kopyčincy
Sanok Star.Sambor 31 Zidačev Rogatin Monastyriska 17
Lesko Ustrzyki DROHOBYCZ Stryj 14 Burštyn Galič Čortkov 21 Borščev
Cisha Din. Borislav СТРЫЙ 23 Kaluš 20 28 Tlumač Kam.Po
Ruské БОРИСЛАВ 37 Bolechov 16 29 32 295 Gorodenka 24 Zaleščiki КАМ.ПОД
umenné Turka Skole Dolina STANIS- 34 Otynja 36 Kolomyja Snjatyn 49
ranov Borinja 220 Pereginskoje LAWOW Deljatin КОЛОМЫЯ 42 ČERNOV
ovce 30 Vel.Bereznyj 89 Solotvin Nadvornaja 35 Rožnov 35 ЧЕР
Sečovce 39 Perečin Volovec Kremincy 30 Berégomet ČERNOVO
Treblšov Užgorod Mežgorje 25 Jasinja Storožlnec
20 ljaujhely УЖГОРОД Svaljava Kušnica Verchovina Krasnoil'sk Porubno
Kisvárda 23 42 Mukačevo Ust' Dubovoje 29 Putila Putna
22 Cop 24 МУКАЧЕВО Corna Seljatin Moldovița
Székely 27 50 Beregovo 65 Chust Rachov Gu
21 44 5 ХУСТ 27 Tjačev 72 Cimpulung Humo
gyh'za Matészalka Halmeu Sighet ul Marmaț. Vişuel de Sus Iacobeni Mol
32 20 15 Negrești 15 Glulești Săcel 26 15
20 19 Satu Mare 50 51 Cavnic Moiselu Rodna Vatra Dor
Hajdúhadház Nyirbátor Carei 37 Ardușat Baia Mare 38 Telclu Poiana Poiana T
Valea 36 Benesat Năsăud Stampei
DEBRECEN 18 Marghita Răstoci 58 Bistrița 12 Deda 42 Toplita
110Pocsal Simlăul- Dej 15 55 Sărățel 50 Ioseni
ökládány 41 Săcueni Silvaniel Zalău Romănași Gherla Tagu Reghin Sovata
34 Berettyóújfalu 35 Alesd 43 31 50 Apahida Prald Ml
8.harkeresztes 18 Clucea 23 Huedin 15 Cămărașu Sovata
eghalom 37 ORADEA Roșia 54 268 CLUJ- 31 Turda Tg. Mureș 21 Bălăușeri
Salonta Celca 31 Belus NAPOCA 21 50 34 32
Sarkad 25 Ripa Buru Iernut
117 Bells 28 37